# Dive Into

# ACTION!

## For Recent Graduates

Don't Be **A Part Of** the Pack,
Be **Apart From** the Pack!

# Gary Lim

**DORATO PRESS**

Dedicated to my wife Judy and our daughter,

both of whom keep me looking ahead

to what can be, and what will be.

FIRST EDITION

Publisher's Cataloging-in-Publication Data

Lim, Gary.

Dive into action! for recent graduates; don't be a part of the pack, be apart from the pack! / Gary Lim.: -- 1st ed.

p. ; cm.

ISBN: 978-0-578-07569-3

1. Career development.  2. Job hunting--United States.  3. Unemployed--Psychology.  I. Title.

HF5381 .L563 2011

650.14                                                        2010942708

For further information:
315-885-1532
www.ActionPronto.com
www.BooksByGaryLim.com

**Also by Gary Lim**


**Dive Into ACTION!**
Find Your Niche in Times of Uncertainty


**Let It Fly!**
Defy the Laws of Business Gravity and
Keep Your Company Soaring


**The Road to Gumption**
Using Your Inner Courage To Balance
Your Work and Personal Life

# Introduction

This work is an adaptation of my well-received third book, *Dive Into ACTION! Find Your Niche in Times of Uncertainty*, which has been a helpful resource for many professionals in the workplace who find themselves looking for their next great opportunity. That book was focused mostly on people who have been in the workplace for a number of years or more.

But what about you, the recent or soon-to-be graduate from an institution of higher education? Every year, approximately 2.5 million degrees are earned: associate, bachelor's, master's, professional, and doctorate. Many of the degrees are earned part-time by people who are already employed, but everyone else will need to seek positions upon graduation. Add to that the number of people currently unemployed in the U.S., and you have a challenging job market.

Don't be discouraged by the numbers. There are still many opportunities at "entry level" positions and above, and although many open positions get filled, the candidate pool will be very competitive. The key is getting a company to understand your value to them. You will need to become very good at making yourself stand out from the crowd at every stage, to:

- get a phone screen
- be invited to an initial interview
- go back for a second round of interviews, and
- get that job offer.

Don't be a part of the pack, **be apart from the pack**. To make this happen, take ACTION:

**A** is for **Accomplishments**

**C** is for **Connect**

**T** is for **Target**

**I** is for **Implement**

**O** is to be **Objective**

**N** is for **Nerves**

Master these phases of your job search, and you will maximize your chances of finding an opportunity that you seek. It won't be easy, and there are no guarantees, but what choice do you have? After all, we're talking about your career, so why wouldn't you give it your all?

In this book I'll share with you my perspective on the things you can do that will help you stand out. It's a perspective that I've acquired from a career where I've interviewed and hired many people, and also from competing for positions where there was much competition. I want you to be **apart from** the pack, and not become **a part of** the pack.

Keep reading to find out exactly what you need to do during each of these phases, to maximize your chances in the job market. All the best ... now Dive Into ACTION!

Gary Lim

info@ActionPronto.com
http://myActionPronto.com

# Contents

"Choose a job you love, and you will never have to work
a day in your life."

— Confucius


"All that stands between the graduate and the top of the ladder
is the ladder."

— Author Unknown

# "A" is for Accomplishments

*"Never mistake activity for achievement."*
--John Wooden

One of the first things many students or recent graduates do when searching for a job is to prepare their resumes. They list the positions they had during the summer, or internships held during the school year. And when they describe what they did in each position, they often list as many things as they can to make the position look more substantial. As you prepare your resume by thinking back on what you can put into it, beware of falling into this trap.

It's not about how much you should put into your resume. It's about knowing what should be in your resume, and what shouldn't.

Mistake #1 in this phase ... thinking that what you *did* in a job, is what you *accomplished.* As the quote from legendary UCLA basketball coach John Wooden indicates, "activity" and "achievement" (accomplishments) are two different things. Since most students or recent graduates make this mistake, if you make sure you don't, you stand to be apart from the pack.

So what should you put in? The answer is, as many "accomplishments" as you can think of, and as few "activities" as possible. Accomplishments are things that you achieved that have an effect on people or situations. Activities are merely what you did to pass the time of day while you were working.

Granted, all jobs are made up of activities of one type or another, but it's what resulted from those activities, the impact of those activities, that potential employers are more interested in than the activities themselves. Allow me show you what I mean with a hypothetical example.

Let's say one of your summer jobs was being a camp counselor at a local camp in the mountains. It consisted of the usual collection of duties that a camp counselor would have, maybe leading group activities for the kids, organizing short outings, and helping to serve the meals. If you just listed these items on your resume, you would be merely listing activities.

What employers will find more interesting is the impact these activities had, on the kids, on the camp, and even on you. And if you can connect the dots for them and show them how your activities made you a better person, made the kids better kids, or made the camp a better camp, that's what employers really want to know about you.

So maybe because you led group activities, the way you did it allowed the kids in camp to learn more independence and become more self-starting. Or because you organized some of the outings for the entire camp, you sharpened your organizational skills and became much better at coordinating different aspects of a bigger picture. Or maybe in the course of helping to serve some of the meals, you made some suggestions that helped mealtimes progress smoothly and with very few hitches.

Get the picture? If you merely list activities, employers will not always have the time to figure out what the impact of your activities were. You might think that it's obvious, and that they should be able to figure it out, but they won't have time to spend on it. It's easier for them to move on to the next resume to see if there's anything interesting that jumps out from that one.

What if you think you had a job that's routine, and you don't think there's much impact from it? A major grocery store not far from where I live employs lots of students in summer or part-time positions, working as check-out cashiers. I'm sure a lot of these students think that they wouldn't be able to list any accomplishments that would sound interesting, because all they did all day was scan the customers' groceries, pack them, and collect payment.

If you had one of these positions, you might think the same. And, in fact, if all you did was scan the customers' groceries, pack them, and collect payment, and nothing else, then it would be routine, and you'd be a part of the pack.

But you want to be *apart from* the pack, so if you had that job you should have been looking for ways to make your experience fuller. Maybe you'd be asking your supervisor if you could experience a couple of different departments during the summer, not just the cashier line. Or maybe you'd ask her if you could sit in on a company training class or seminar, perhaps even on your own time.

Employers want to know how your past positions impacted you, the company you worked for, and the people you worked with. If you can describe your positions in those terms, you're well on your way to being apart from the pack. Most of the other candidates who are competing for the same positions as you, are not doing this.

This is the mindset I want you to get into, thinking "accomplishments" and "impact" instead of "activities". It's so important, I want to place this sticky note here to remind you.

Think "accomplishments" and "impact", not "activities", when you think about your past jobs.

It involves some thought, but remember, this is about setting you apart from the pack, to get invited to those phone screens and interviews. So here's what I want you to do, to turn your list of summer jobs and internships into accomplishments:

**Step 1**. On a sheet of paper, or in a new Microsoft Word document (or other PC, Mac, or web-based word processing application of your choice), list the companies or organizations where you held your most recent internships, part-time, or summer jobs, latest positions first. Using any word processing application would make things easier, since you will be inserting new information in between the lines.

**Step 2**. Under each company/organization name, enter a job title that best describes what you did. If you were working for a company or other organization, you probably had a job title like "Retail Sales Clerk", "Receptionist", "Computer Technician", etc. If you held an internship, you might or might not have had a specific title, but you could use "Business Intern", "Engineering Intern", or other title you choose that fits the function you served.

**Step 3**. Start with the most recent position first. Under your title for the job, make a list of things you did in that position while you were there. You can list ongoing, repetitive "day-to-day" duties (e.g. answering phones, responding to customer service emails), and also any special projects you worked on during that time. List whatever comes to mind, and for now don't worry about how many items you have in your list.

**Step 4**. For each item in your list, answer the following question about how that duty, activity, or project helped the company, your co-workers, or the customers:

*So what?*

For example, say you were working at a computer service company one summer. In your list of activities, you might have listed that you "serviced, repaired, and optimized clients' computers."

*So what?*

Maybe you serviced those computers faster than the clients expected. They were hoping to get their systems back in one week, and you were able to get them returned to them in 3 days. Net result, a pleasantly surprised customer.

Or maybe you took each computer and ran optimization scripts on them, then looked at their directory structures to see how things might be improved.

*So what?*

Bottom line, the systems on average ran 25% faster after you got done with them, and the customers were again pleasantly surprised.

And perhaps another activity was the owner of the firm asking you to give him some feedback on the process in the shop. You studied the flow and made some recommendations.

*So what?*

The owner took some of your suggestions, and the result was a shorter turnaround time for systems to be completed. In fact, your suggestions reduced the average time a system spent in the shop by about one-third.

Get the idea? Take every activity, duty, or project that you've listed under your job title, and think of how your customers, company, or co-workers were positively affected by your efforts. If you can, express those positive impacts quantitatively, such as "increased by a factor of 2", or "cut the time spent in half", or "doubled the number of customers served", etc.

What you're doing is answering the "so what?" question by listing the benefits of what you did. Enter the benefit below the listed activity it corresponds to. If you're using word processing, change the color of that text to green.

**Step 5**. Look over your green list of benefits, the answers to the "so what?" question. Pick the 3 or 4 that seem to suggest the largest impact, and use them in your resume for the description of what you did in that position. By describing your activities in terms of benefits or accomplishments, instead of just activities, you set yourself apart from the pack. You also help "connect the dots" for those interested in knowing more about you, as to what you might be able to do for them.

Keep this "green list" in mind whenever you get interviewed about your previous jobs. It will help your interviewer see how you were able to add value to your position, and that's what can really catch their attention.

# Summary — "A" is for "Accomplishments"

Think accomplishments, not activities. It's not just about what you've done, but more about the impact and value of what you've done.

Use the 5-step process and the "so what?" question to take your activities and emphasize how they brought value and benefit to where you worked. How did your job tasks bring benefits to:

- Customers

- The company

- Your own skills

Focus on these benefits to connect the dots for readers of your resume.

Keep your list of accomplishments and examples of impact in mind, for when you get interviewed for possible jobs.

# "C" is for Connect

*"Lots of people want to ride with you in the limo,*
*but what you want is someone who will take the bus with you*
*when the limo breaks down."*
-- Oprah Winfrey

You've probably already heard this – when you're looking for a job in a competitive market, your job becomes to find that job. This will take the involvement of others; you can't do it all yourself. You also can't expect others to do it all for you, either.

In my work and travels, I hear far too many job seekers say that they're waiting on other people to get back to them. Or that so-and-so was going to introduce them to someone they know. Or that they've sent in their resume but they haven't heard from anyone.

The problem with these statements is that the candidate appears to be waiting for someone else to take action – to get back to them, or to make the introduction. You're the job seeker – set yourself apart from the pack and take the active role.

Waiting for someone to get back to you? Give them a call and ask if they have any other questions, or if there's something you can do to help their review of your application.

Did someone else say he would introduce you to someone he knows, but you haven't heard back from your contact yet? Call or email him, and tell him you'd be happy to reach out to the other person directly if he'll share the contact information.

Sent in a resume, but haven't heard from anyone? Find out who to call, make the call, and ask if there are any early questions you can answer.

Don't be a part of the pack, by waiting for others to contact you. Be apart from the pack – take action and make the call, send the email, or reach out in some other way.

Since it takes the involvement of others to connect and find a job, involve others whenever you can. Tell everyone you know, that you're looking for a job, and maybe even some people you don't know yet. Don't be bashful. Spread the word.

But here's the catch…

There are plenty of people in your situation who aren't afraid of spreading the word that they are looking for a job. However, most of them do not succeed in articulating the type of job they're looking for, so one or more of the following results:

1. It comes across as if they will look at any job that comes their way.

2. It comes across as if they will look at only a select few jobs, like they're being picky.

3. No one gets a clear picture of what the job seeker is looking for.

4. No one gets a clear picture of what the job seeker would be good at doing.

Your job, as you connect with everyone you know, is to make it easy for them to remember what you could be good at, and what you're looking for. Don't forget, make it "easy" and "memorable" for the person you're communicating with. To do that, you need…

An elevator pitch.

Often used more by start-up companies pitching for investment capital, the elevator pitch is a short, memorable speech that tells the listener the high points of the start-up, its target market, key products, and benefits. The pitch is designed to entice the listener (in the case of start-ups, the prospective investor) to learn more during a follow-up conversation or meeting. But the elevator pitch has to be short enough and memorable, because it's usually delivered in a venue where the listener is not able to take notes, and where there might be many other people delivering their pitches as well.

For you, the concept of an elevator pitch can be an effective tool that you can use for your job search. The key product you're pitching is **you**. The benefits are to potential companies in search of talented individuals like you.

Bottom line, you need to construct an elevator pitch about yourself, in answer to a question like "What are your plans after you get your degree?", or "What type of job are you looking for?"

If you have a simple, understandable elevator pitch in response, you will maximize the chance of that listener remembering what you're seeking and why you can bring value to a company or other organization. If you're not exactly sure what you're seeking, that's okay, but you should at least have a clear idea of what you're good at and why you can contribute.

This circles back to the list of accomplishments or impact that you created in the first phase, the "A" in ACTION. That list (in green font) of your accomplishments or impact is what I consider to be the value you can bring to a company. Pick the top 2 most important or memorable, to use in your elevator pitch.

Here's how to construct your pitch. Use the following outline to get started, but feel free to vary the wording to fit your style and personality. Your elevator pitch will have four main sections:

1. Education
2. Position
3. Value
4. Closing

The first section, on education, has this general format:

**"I am majoring in _____ at _____ and will be graduating with my degree in _____."**

You fill in your major, your college or university, and the month and year of your graduation date.

The next section, on the position you're seeking, goes like this:

**"Right now I'm interested in looking for a position in the _____ industry, perhaps as a _____ or a _____."**

You add the name of the industry you're interested in, and one or two position titles or roles that you would consider in your job search, positions that you can see yourself in.

(At this point, it's okay if you don't have a definitive idea of what to put in the blanks. You will, more so, after we cover the "T" in ACTION in the next chapter.)

The third section of the elevator pitch is where you speak to the value that you bring to a company, despite not having years and years of experience. Or, if you do have years and years of experience, this is where you can allude to it. The general format is:

**"I think I can contribute to any company because in past jobs, I've demonstrated the ability to _____, which at one company resulted in _____. At another company, I _____, resulting in _____."**

You add the skill that you demonstrated at that past position, and the impact or accomplishment that resulted. Remember your list of accomplishments in green font? Refer to that. If you have a second, compelling example to use, use it, but if not, stick with just one strong example.

The fourth and final part of your elevator pitch is the closing. Now that you've told them about your strengths, ask them to keep you in mind:

**"If you hear about any positions that might seem like it would be a fit, I'd appreciate it if you would let me know."**

And with that, you hand them your business card.

What business card, you ask? The one that you've printed with your name, mailing address, phone number, and email address on it. Go to Kinko's, Staples, or any other printing place and have some made up. They don't have to be fancy. They can be on plain white cardstock, with professional font that's easy to read. Or, if you have a good enough inkjet printer, you can print your own on blank cardstock that you can buy at Staples or at other office supply stores.

But please – no artsy fonts like decorative or script fonts that are hard to decipher. These can be annoying. Also remember that some of the people you give your card to might be members of the generation that uses reading glasses, so be sure to make your fonts large enough to be read easily.

Having a business card for your job search is a handy tool. When you deliver your elevator pitch somewhere, it's not likely that you're going to hand the listener a resume, unless they ask for one. Even then, you might not have a resume handy, especially if you happen to be in the aisle of a local grocery store or the corner hardware store at home.

But you can always have your business cards handy, in your wallet or purse, ready to give out at a moment's notice. And if the listener does ask if you happen to have a resume, you could ask for her card, and tell her that you will mail it to her.

If she doesn't have a business card handy, take out another one of yours and write her information down on the back of it.

Putting this all together, here's how one possible elevator pitch might sound:

**"I am majoring in chemical engineering at Blue Skies University, and will be graduating with my bachelor's degree in May 201x. Right now I'm interested in looking for a position in the pharmaceutical industry, perhaps as an entry level analyst or chemical engineer.**

**"I think I can contribute to any company, because in past jobs I've demonstrated the ability to come up to speed quickly. At one company, after being there for only one month, my suggestions resulted in a 10% increase in sales of one of the product lines.**

**"If you hear about any positions that might seem like it would be a fit for me, I'd appreciate it if you would let me know. May I give you one of my cards?"**

One more thing, once you construct your elevator pitch. Practice it, practice some more, then practice even more. You should have it so well practiced that you could give it flawlessly even if I woke you up from a deep sleep at 3 o'clock in the morning.

So, put together your elevator pitch, and rehearse it until it is second nature. Print your business cards, put on a smile, and go out and connect with everyone you know.

And maybe even some you don't know yet.

# Summary – "C" is for "Connect"

In the "C" of ACTION, you need to connect with everyone you know, and maybe some you don't know yet, regarding your search for a job.

Create your elevator pitch, with the 4 essential sections:

1) Education

2) Position

3) Value

4) Closing

After you create your pitch, practice it until it becomes almost instinctive. It's okay to hone it over time as you see ways to improve it, but be sure you have your pitch well-rehearsed. I should be able to wake you up at 3 o'clock in the morning and hear the perfectly delivered pitch.

Now, deliver your pitch any opportunity you get. And go print some business cards to hand out afterward, so they can keep you in mind in case they run across anything interesting for you.

# "T" is for "Target"

*"Concentrate all your thoughts upon the work at hand.*
*The sun's rays do not burn until brought to a focus."*

-- Alexander Graham Bell

In this "T" phase of the acronym ACTION, you create a plan for your job search ... you figure out what types of jobs, and companies or organizations, to target. This effort will also help you write and refine the 2nd element of your elevator pitch, as I discussed in the previous chapter.

Ask yourself the following questions and take some notes:

- What industries are you interested in?

- What are some of the roles you can see yourself in?

- What are some of the things you like doing?

- What are some things you don't particularly like doing?

Let's cover each of these 4 questions.

Think about what industries you've been interested in, that you can relate your college experience to. Make a note of 2 or 3 industries that you would find interesting, like pharmaceuticals, manufacturing, software, or retail, as some examples.

Next, for each of the industries that you listed, imagine 1 or 2 roles you could see yourself filling within those industries. If it's the retail industry for example, do you see yourself dealing with customers, or working in the back office in some capacity? If it's in pharmaceuticals, do you think you would want to be a sales representative, calling on doctors, or do you want to work in a lab? If it's in manufacturing, do you want to work with the production line in some way, or would you rather work with the supply chain? Make a note of those possible roles underneath the industry you've listed.

For the 3rd question, think about what you like doing. Do you like dealing with people? Do you like crunching numbers? Writing software routines? Working outdoors? Fixing computer systems? Solving complex problems? Create a list of these things. The items on the list don't have to be mutually exclusive. For example, if you like working outdoors and fixing computer systems, make a note of both.

For the last question, turn it around the other way – think about the things you don't particularly like doing. Do you hate working outdoors? Don't particularly like working with the public? Not good on the phone? Is writing your nemesis? Rather not work in an office setting? Make a list of these items.

Now you're ready to start laying out your targets. Go back to the list of industries you're interested in, and review the roles you see yourself in. Starting with the first industry you noted, start researching and finding out about the companies that are in that industry. Organize a list of your findings – whether you use a Microsoft Office product like Word, Excel, or Access, or another software application on the PC, Mac, or web-based, it's your choice. But use something that makes it easy to record and review your findings over time.

As you come across or read about new companies in your chosen industries, add them to your list.

For each company you add to your list, read enough about it to familiarize yourself with the company from this perspective:

- What business is the company in? A few product lines, or many?

- Who are the main customer groups that the firm sells to?

- What is the firm's strategy for growing its market share?

- How does the company view itself? What sets it apart from its competitors?

- Do they appear to be hiring? Are there any specific job openings?

Add notes on each company to the appropriate place in the organized list of your findings. Build a "dossier" or set of notes for each company on your list. Have it set up so you can easily go back and refer to the information you gathered on the firm. You are building your own database of information on companies that you will target during your job search.

If you have more than one industry that you're interested in, you will find that you'll have multiple groups of companies to pursue. As you build your plan of attack, you would tailor your approach depending on which group you're pursuing a position with.

The best way for me to illustrate "tailoring an approach" is to briefly reminisce back to my own job search as I was completing my undergraduate degree, which was in electrical engineering and computer science. It was some time ago, but the analogy is still valid. I ended up in final interviews for positions in 3 distinct groups of companies:

- Large industrials like General Electric and Westinghouse Electric

- Computer systems firms like IBM and Hewlett Packard

- Aircraft companies, like Boeing Corporation and Grumman Aerospace (which years later became Northrup Grumman)

Not only were my interview pursuits in 3 different industry groups, but the type of work I would be doing differed with each group as well. In the large industrials like GE and Westinghouse, I would have had some kind of technical analyst or systems engineering role, utilizing the analytical perspective of my engineering education, but probably not my computer science concentration.

At the computer companies of IBM and HP, I was pursuing jobs that were in technical marketing. So, while my computer science studies were relevant to the product line, my work would likely utilize relatively little of my engineering education. Finally, at the aircraft companies of Boeing and Grumman, my work probably would have been technical or analytical in nature and applied to the aircraft/aerospace industry, but not necessarily related to my field of study in college.

My strategy was based on applying a slightly different approach, depending on which group of companies I was interviewing with. And remember, the IBM and HP opportunities were for marketing positions and not engineering.

I was fortunate enough to land multiple job offers at the time, and ultimately decided that I wanted to start my career in a marketing and business capacity, so I went to HP as the first stop in my career. I recognized the things that I enjoyed, such as working with outside customers and seeing the "big picture" of business. Even though my position at HP was entry-level, it offered those things.

Bottom line for you in your search … answer the 4 questions at the beginning of this chapter, then start building your database of companies to target your job search at. Have an approach in mind depending on the type of company you're targeting.

Though this chapter is about setting up a company prospect database and a plan, it's a dynamic process. Remember that you shouldn't wait until you complete your database before you start contacting firms. Set up your plan to run parallel tracks: contact companies, apply for open positions, make connections, keep finding new companies, and do it all over again.

If things change in the industries or companies you have targeted, make changes to your plan if needed. Be sure to keep up on any new developments that affect the companies in your database.

The more you know about your targeted firms, the more you are likely to set yourself apart from the pack.

# Summary – "T" is for "Target"

Answer the 4 questions at the beginning of this chapter, to focus on your interests and strengths. Once you decide on what industries and job types interest you, you can target your search accordingly.

Within each industry of interest, identify companies where you can research opportunities. Look at firms of all sizes, large, medium and small.

Find as many companies as you can. Get to know them, and build your database.

Put your target firms into groups if appropriate, that might require different approaches when prospecting and interviewing. Match your strengths and experience to the approach of each group of companies.

Keep adding newly uncovered companies to your target list and research them. Don't stop until you have found and accepted a job.

# "I" is for "Implement"

*"Nothing will work unless you do."*
--Maya Angelou

So you've formulated the plan for your job search, based on your interest in 1, 2, or even 3 industries. And you've imagined yourself in different roles within each industry, and have researched the web and other places to learn about companies in those industries.

You've searched the listings at the most popular job listing websites, including but not limited to Yahoo! hotjobs, CareerBuilder.com, Monster.com, Indeed, SimplyHired, and others. You've also looked at individual company websites to view any of their openings.

The only thing to do next is to dive right in. Implement your plan, work your database, expand your database, and repeat the cycle.

Let's look at 8 things you should be doing in this "Implement" stage:

1. Apply for positions appearing on a job listing website (e.g. Monster.com), relevant to your search at companies that you have already researched

2. Apply for a position listed on the website of a specific company you have researched

3. Continue to search for new listings on job websites

4. Continue to search for new companies to add to your industries of interest

5. Research and learn about the new companies uncovered in the process of doing #3 and #4.

6. Call, email, or write to follow up on open applications you put in.

7. Call, email, or write to establish contact with someone at a company that you're interested in learning more about.

8. Any other call, email, or other form of communication that supports your ongoing job search effort, including calls to introduce yourself to someone new.

There are a number of ways to work this list of 8 tasks, but you might want to consider a couple of approaches.

One approach is to go through the list of 8 tasks every day, checking if you have any actions to take in each of the numbered items. Depending on what's happening, this could make for a bit of a jumbled day.

Another approach is to take the numbered items and only do certain ones depending on the day of the week. You might have noticed that of the 8 tasks, there are 3 categories:

- Category "A": creating/submitting the job application – task #1, #2;

- Category "B": researching company information – #3, #4, #5

- Category "C": making contact for the purpose of follow-up or networking – #6, #7, #8.

You could decide to work on certain task categories only on certain days, for example:

- Monday: category A and C

- Tuesday: category B

- Wednesday: category B and C

- Thursday: category A, B and C

- Friday: category B

In this example scenario, I have you completing and submitting applications on Monday and Thursday, researching companies and jobs every day except Monday, and making contact on Monday, Wednesday, and Thursday. By the way, "making contact" also includes all the time you spend attempting to make contact, like participating in "telephone tag" or just making repeated attempts to reach the person.

The reason for taking this approach is that it sometimes makes it a bit easier to focus on what you need to do that day. If you're submitting a job application, online or not, you need to have a certain mindset to focus on what you'll include in your application and your cover letter, if that's a part of it too. If you're making or returning calls, you'll need to be in a different mindset. Research is the only mode where it's easier to resume after being interrupted.

Whichever method you choose, you should also pick a day where you perform "housekeeping" tasks, such as straightening out your desk, cleaning up your notes from conversations where you didn't have a chance to complete them earlier, etc. During the times when I was in job searches, I usually did this on Fridays, because there wasn't as much going on otherwise.

During this stage you should continue to connect with people as you started to in the "Connect" stage of ACTION. Be sure your elevator pitch has been honed to a high level, and that you know it almost instinctively because you've rehearsed it so extensively.

There's also a lot of discussion these days about the use of social media to connect with people you might not know. If you're interested in that, there are many books, articles, and other resources on the topic of using social media to search for jobs. But my view has remained the same over time, that connections are made between people, and nothing will replace the need to meet in person, or at least talk live by telephone.

Don't be discouraged by delays or lack of response to your calls, letters, or emails. The news reports are filled with job seekers being quoted that they never heard back from anyone they contacted. That's a fact, that most firms will not have the time to proactively contact candidates just to tell them that their application or email was received.

However …

If you make it easy for them, most people will be willing to talk with you. That's where following up will set you apart from the pack. Most of the pack just sits and waits to hear. By following up, you have the opportunity to get your name to rise above. There's no guarantee that you'll be able to reach the person you're trying to reach, but if you do, by definition you've set yourself apart.

Some job seekers feel that they don't want to be a pest. There is a fine line between being a pest, and being persistent. If you follow up politely but persistently, the person you're trying to reach is unlikely to be put off by it.

If you figure you won't be a pest and wait for them to get back to you, in most cases you will probably wait for a very long time. Make notes about when you call or email, so you know when you can make your next call or send another email without being pesky.

Years ago I pursued a contact in a company, with the hope of doing some joint work. I called the contact periodically, maybe 3 or 4 times a year, and sent her information once or twice a year. Most of the time, I received no response. This went on for literally 5 *years*, and over that period of time, I spoke with the contact a total of 3 or 4 times, only when I happened to catch her at her desk. When the time was right and we finally worked on a project together, she thanked me for staying in touch and being persistent. It turned out to be a good partnership, and she was appreciative of the fact that I hung in there for so long, trying to make it happen.

The point I'm emphasizing here is that following up with someone, as long as it's done courteously, is almost always appreciated. You're making it easier for them because it's one less thing for them to remember to do. Keep in mind that it's not their responsibility to think about calling you back or even contacting you at all.

Before leaving the "I" stage of ACTION, I want to remind you that it's okay to take a break from the grind once in awhile. The "I" stage can sometimes be a drag, where you're just trying to grind stuff out. Even though it's your job for now, there is nothing wrong with taking a little time off.

If things are a little slow, and you don't expect to reach anyone on a particular day, consider taking the day off to do something that gives your mind a break — it could be something as simple as walking around your local mall for a couple of hours.

# Summary – "I" is for "Implement"

Review the 8 things you do in the "I" stage of ACTION, and decide how you want to divvy them up in your schedule. There are 3 categories of tasks to consider.

Take those tasks and schedule them for specific days of the week. Experiment with the schedule in the beginning, but as you get to know your work habits, settle in with a schedule that you know you can keep. And be sure to stick to it.

Be persistent but polite in your follow-up. Don't assume that they'll remember to get back to you – make it easy for them by contacting them first. This will set you apart from the pack.

Take a break from the grind now and then. Get your mind off of things, and do something that you enjoy. Then get back to work, and work your target company list.

# "O" is to be "Objective"

*"Stay committed to your decisions, but*
*stay flexible in your approach."*
--Tony Robbins

I've been doing a lot of talking about setting your strategy, targets, and action items, then implementing them to reach your objectives. In this "O" stage of ACTION, the meaning of the word "objective" that I refer to is the one where you try to remain impartial – where you stay objective in your viewpoint.

This perspective is needed if you are fortunate enough to be in the position of trying to decide between multiple job offers. But these are also useful thoughts to have in mind even if you only have one offer on the table.

Let's start by discussing the first of the two situations – where you have two offers, from two different companies, to choose from. Furthermore, we'll assume that the timing of both offers is similar, i.e. you have about the same amount of time to decide and your decision due dates are about the same. But to make it a little more challenging, let's say that both base salaries are fair, but one of the salary offers is 10% higher.

This is a great situation. You've got two companies that want you to join them, and one of them is offering a salary 10% higher than the other. Might as well take the extra money, right?

Not so fast. This is where you need to remember that "O" is to be "Objective". Job opportunities are not only about the amount of money you'll be making. There are a number of other aspects that you might find just as important as, or even more important than, the size of your base salary. For example, consider these factors:

- Strength and outlook of the company

- Company culture

- Opportunity for advancement

- Location of the job, and the cost of living

- Opportunity to grow your skills, e.g. management training programs, tuition reimbursement

- Fringe benefits, such as health, dental, vision, fitness center

- Other sources of income, such as employee profit sharing, employee stock purchase plan, employee bonus plan

- When it's all said and done, will you like working there?

You can consider each factor in the form of several questions you ask yourself, if you are considering an offer from a company or organization. Here are some of the questions you ought to be asking, and if you can't find the answers with your own research, ask the person extending you the offer. Even if you research your own answers, you should ask anyway.

*Strength and outlook of the company.* Is the company in good financial shape? Is it poised for growth in a good economy, or at least holding its own in a down economy? Does it seem like it's able to afford the things it needs to do to grow? Is the market that it serves a stable market, or one that goes through extreme ups and downs?

*Company culture.* Does the organization or company value its employees? (Most companies say they do, but is it really the case?) Do people work long hours because they're busy, or because everyone works long hours? These are questions you can ask the people who you interviewed with, when the time is right.

*Opportunity for advancement.* If you did really well with the job you're being offered, does it seem like there is room for you to grow your career with the organization? Or is that really the only job you're going to have as long as you stay with the firm?

*Location of the job, and cost of living.* Let's say the job with the 10% higher salary is located in a major metropolitan area while the other job is not. "Major metropolitan" would be cities like New York, Boston, Washington, D.C., San Francisco, Chicago, and other major population areas. Suddenly, the 10% difference might not be that much of a difference at all, depending on how much more it will cost you to rent an apartment or buy a house there. In fact, you could end up with less money in your pocket after you factor in the other aspects like utilities, gas, and food. But you might not care, because you might still want the experience of working in a major metro area, so that could override the financial disadvantage if there is one.

*Opportunity to grow your skills.* This is related to, but separate from, opportunity for advancement. Are there training courses that you can enroll in, to hone your management skills, or other skill sets? Is there a tuition reimbursement program for an advanced degree that you'd like to earn?

*Fringe benefits.* Sometimes a company will offer a higher salary but have less coverage in terms of healthcare benefits, compared to another firm that has a lower salary but more complete coverage. Be sure to understand the true picture of both offers in this regard.

*Other sources of income.* Does the company have a bonus plan or employee profit-sharing plan? If so, what has that plan typically paid, and to what might that translate, dollar-wise, in terms of the position that you're considering? If the firm is a public company (NYSE or NASDAQ), is there an employee stock purchase plan? Some public firms allow their employees to buy stock at an average price minus an employee discount. That can translate to a financial advantage as well.

If the company is a start-up looking for outside investment capital, are they offering you a stock option? There are no guarantees that the stock will be worth anything, but having a stock option is a potential "upside" to supplement a salary that is not at the high end of the spectrum.

*Will you like working there?* When it's all said and done, and you've looked at all the other non-salary factors of the offer, you have to ask yourself if you envision yourself working there, and enjoying it. No matter how much money you get paid, if you don't like what you're doing, or where you're doing it, either you or your employer will eventually want you to leave.

Bottom line, if you're fortunate enough to be entertaining two (or more) offers, that's great. Be sure to think about more than just the salary level. There are a whole host of other factors that can change your view on the differences in salaries between the offers.

What about if you're considering an offer, without another one to compare it to? This might be more the common situation. You should still look at the offer with an objective eye, with the possibility of turning it down to wait on other possibilities.

That's right, I mean the "possibility" of turning the offer down. I'm not advocating that you turn it down, but I'm also not necessarily saying that you accept an offer just because it's the only one you have on the table. It's not easy turning down a job offer in favor of being unemployed, but you should at least look at the longer-term view and consider the effects.

Let's say the offer you received is for a job that you interviewed for, but perhaps wasn't your favorite, top-of-the-list opportunity. But, you figure it's a job. And maybe you're even thinking, I'll continue to look for a better job after I start this one.

Don't go down that path.

Unless the job you're taking is truly a "temporary" style position, where the employer only wants temporary instead of full-time help, it's not a good practice to take a job with the intent of looking for another one. Most employers will have a problem with you taking their money in salary, even if you're performing your assigned duties, but casting a wandering eye toward other job openings. That's the first problem.

The second problem is that if you're not that energized by what you're doing, or worse, not even interested in what you're doing, then it will show up in your job performance. That is a certainty. It may not appear until 3 months from now, 6 months, or even a year, but it will appear – I guarantee it. And when your job performance takes a dip, that could even cost you your job, and you'll be back where you started.

Actually, you'll be worse off than where you started, because you'll have to explain why you didn't stay at your last job very long. And the references you will need from that last position might not be the strongest or the most glowing ones.

So unless you're in dire financial straits and absolutely need to bring in cash now, you'd be wise to take a little extra time to cast an objective eye at the offer, even if it's the only one you have. There might be other opportunities you're looking at that are more ideal, but are taking longer than you expected. If one of those materializes, that could be closer to the "perfect job" that you seek.

Then again, those other opportunities might not come your way at all. That's the difficult part, not knowing if your other pursuits will bear fruit. You will likely end up making a decision that's partly a guess, but at least look the offer over with objective eyes.

Speaking of the "perfect job" – there isn't one. Be flexible. All job offers have pluses and minuses. No exceptions. Just be sure you understand what the pluses and minuses are, and that the pluses outweigh the minuses before you accept an offer.

Are you wondering why anyone would ever turn down a job, without another offer on the table? Years ago, I did, once. I was in between companies, and seeking a management position. At my level, the opportunities were fewer in number, by definition.

I was offered a position with a company that fit the profile of what I was looking for, with one exception. The company's product line was not particularly interesting to me. I was worried that if I took the position, after a year my lack of interest in the product line might show. I had no doubt that I could perform my job duties better than anyone else, but I worried that my performance would suffer if I wasn't motivated by the industry I would have been in.

So I did the scary thing and turned down the position, even though I didn't have any other offers to consider. I had applications submitted at other companies, but none of those were at the point of being close to an offer yet. And of course, I had no guarantees that any of those would actually result in an offer.

I looked at the situation by being as objective as I possibly could, and in the end that was the decision I thought was best. Sometime later, one of the other opportunities materialized into an offer that was much closer to what I was seeking.

I'm not saying that I recommend you do the same thing. That is, not unless you have thought it all the way through, and have considered all your other possibilities. You have to make the decision that you're most comfortable with, since you're the one who has to live with it.

# Summary – "O" is to be "Objective"

The hardest thing to do is to be objective about a job offer that you've been working hard to get. But you must.

If you have simultaneous offers, consider more than just the salary. Look at all of the non-salary factors of each offer, and weigh each in the long-term view of things. Understand and recognize which factors are most important to you, and listen to your heart.

Even if you only have one offer on the table, look at it as objectively as you can. Consider the entire picture, and look for that job to be able to help you start or continue your career journey in the right direction.

You will never have enough clear information that will point you to the right decision. But if you take the time to look at the situation objectively, you'll probably have enough clues to trust your instincts.

# "N" is for "Nerves"

*"I get nervous when I don't get nervous. If I'm nervous
I know I'm going to have a good show."*
--Beyonce Knowles

As singer-songwriter Beyonce recognizes, nerves keep you on your toes, and keep your adrenaline flowing. Others have said, nerves mean you care. With this stage of the ACTION acronym, be reassured that it's okay to be nervous. In fact, the right amount of nervousness is a good thing.

These are nervous and insecure times, when you're looking for a job. The trick is to take your nervous energy and focus it positively to your advantage. Too much nervous energy, and you'll appear nervous. If you have an interview and are nervous, all you'll do is make your interviewer nervous. Not many people want to hire nervous candidates, because they make everyone around them nervous.

In contrast, if you focus your nervous energy and channel it, instead of being perceived as nervous, you'll come across as having passion and a sense of urgency. And that's why I say having just the right amount of nervous energy, but not too much, is a good thing.

Let's talk about how to deal with nerves. The first step is fundamental but not always easy to execute:

**Don't worry about things that you can't control.**

If you spend too much time worrying about the things you can't control, you have no time left for focusing on the things you can control, like how well prepared you are for your phone interview, or how professional you will look when you show up for your in-person interview. Spend the time figuring out what will set you apart from the pack, and how to communicate that effectively to the person you'll be speaking with.

After you remember that first step, here's the next thing to remember: the best way to overcome nerves is to prepare well, even over-prepare, for the upcoming event, whether it's a

- phone interview

- first-round in-person interview, or

- follow-up interviews.

How do you over-prepare? You go back to your database of prospective companies, and review all of the material that you've collected on the company that you're interviewing with. Read everything that you've put into your database on the company, and return to their website to refresh your memory of what they do. Try to remember everything you can about the company.

Take the time to think up some good questions you could ask your interviewer, when given the opportunity. I mean good questions … about the company's growth, what its strengths are, what the culture is like, what they're looking for in job candidates. Not questions like how much vacation time do people get, or is there a company cafeteria or gym. The questions you ask should give the interviewer the impression that you're thinking about them, and how you can help the company achieve its goals.

Most candidates in the pack do not prepare well for interviews. The pack tends to tell prospective employers what they, the candidates, are looking for in a company. The pack asks what the company can do for them. Set yourself apart from the pack – tell what you can do for the company, and how you can add value.

The extra preparation you would do to make this impression is how you overcome nerves during interviews. Your nervous energy becomes well-channeled and focused on giving great answers to their questions and asking good questions of your own. The combination of your energy and well-delivered remarks will make it appear that you're enthusiastic about the opportunity, and that you've given it lots of thought. Of course, if you genuinely are enthusiastic about it, you should show it!

In addition to over-preparing for your interviews, deal with your nervousness by finding an outlet through exercise. Go to the gym, lift some weights, go for a run, take a walk, run up and down the stairs in your home. Play tennis, football, soccer, frisbee … anything to burn off that excess nervous energy. It will also make you feel better too, and believe it or not, give you more confidence in your approach.

You don't have to be a gym rat to get into a regimen of regular exercise. And don't worry about being the perfect specimen – that's not what this is all about. You don't even have to belong to a gym. Pick the activity or activities that you know you will stick to, and do them. Make it a part of your routine, like something you must do before you get your day started.

Nerves are good. It means you care. Properly managed, it's one of the advantages that sets you apart from the pack.

# Summary – "N" is for "Nerves"

Simple thought to keep clear in mind – don't worry about things you can't control. Focus on the things you have control over.

To channel your nervous energy for positive results, over-prepare for your phone screens and interviews. Review all you know about the company, and commit as much of that information to memory as you can.

Your knowledge of the target company as they get to know you will give you the confidence and poise to come up with great answers to their questions, and to ask good questions of them. This will go a long way to set you apart from the pack.

Channel your nervous energy by burning it off with regular exercise. Pick the activities you like, and schedule them for a time that you are most likely to keep.

These two methods will make you appear prepared in both mind and body. And what company wouldn't be interested in hiring someone knowledgeable who's done their homework, and who looks like they're ready to rock?

# Final Words

*"Try not. Do or do not. There is no try."*
--Yoda, from the movie *The Empire Strikes Back*

Completing your degree, whether it is an associate's, bachelor's, master's, professional, or doctorate, is a significant milestone. Congratulations – be rightly proud of yourself!

I hope taking ACTION as you embark on the journey to find your next great opportunity will help you stand apart from the pack. You have skills, experience, and potential that would be valuable to many companies and organizations.

The challenge of the job search process is for you to articulate what those skills are, to get the attention of companies as an audience, and to connect the dots, making it easy for them to see how you can add value as an employee.

For some of you, the journey will be quicker than for others. Regardless of the length, make yours a journey during which you discover who you really are, and use that to set yourself apart from the pack.

Now ... Dive Into ACTION!

# ACTION! Summary

A is for **Accomplishments**

C is for **Connect**

T is for **Target**

I is for **Implement**

O is to be **Objective**

N is for **Nerves**

**Accomplishments** are the key, not activities that you've done to pass the time. Be apart from the pack by focusing on your value to organizations you've worked for in the past.

**Connect** with everyone you know. Maybe even some you don't know, yet. Create an elevator pitch, and print some business cards.

**Target** the companies and industries that you're interested in. Dive deep and research all you can find out about them.

**Implement** your action plan. Dive into ACTION! with the 8 things you should be doing.

Be **Objective** before making decisions that affect you over the long-term. The only offer you have is not necessarily the best one.

**Nerves** are good. Channel and focus your nervous energy to look passionate and ready to rock.

# About the Author

Gary Lim, M.A., is Visiting Professor of Entrepreneurship at SUNY College of Environmental Science and Forestry in Syracuse, New York. He is also the founder of ActionPronto.com, the business through which he offers "action plan coaching" services, keynote speaking, and seminars, and president of Aurarius LLC, a management consulting firm he first founded in California's "Silicon Valley" then relocated to Upstate New York. Gary is a co-founder of HealthcareBusinessOffice LLC, and his past business experience includes leadership positions at larger firms such as Hewlett Packard, ROLM, XEROX, and Novell, and at small companies and start-ups.

A seasoned and energetic public speaker, Gary has spoken to audiences in many venues, including keynote addresses, conference workshops, corporate/executive seminars, product launches, and training courses. He has worked with thousands of attendees from organizations ranging from Fortune 500 corporations and mid-market firms to not-for-profits and educational institutions.

As an author, *Dive Into ACTION! for Recent Graduates* is Gary's fourth released work. His first, *The Road to Gumption: Using Your Inner Courage to Balance Your Work and Personal Life* (Dorato Press) was an Amazon #1 Bestseller in its category. Next came *Let It Fly! Defy the Laws of Business Gravity and Keep Your Company Soaring* (Dorato), a business parable featuring effective business leadership principles and a story set at a well-known golf course along the Pacific Ocean. Then came the original *Dive Into ACTION! Find Your Niche in Times of Uncertainty* (Dorato), the book upon which this work is based.

In his work with students, coaching clients, seminar attendees, and at company meetings, Gary is often considered among the best at assessing a complex business or personal situation, identifying the critical issues, and offering practical insight for solutions.

He earned a Bachelor's degree *cum laude* from Princeton University, and a Master's degree in organizational management from University of Phoenix.

To book speaking engagements and seminars, you can find more details on the Web, or contact Gary directly:

| | |
|---|---|
| **Blog:** | http://myActionPronto.com |
| **Website:** | www.ActionPronto.com |
| **Book information:** | www.BooksByGaryLim.com |
| **Email contact:** | info@ActionPronto.com |
| **Phone contact:** | 315-885-1532 |

He can speak more about addressing customized needs, such as:

- Campus seminars
- Keynote speeches
- Breakout sessions
- Volume pricing on books

# Notes

# Notes

# Notes

* 9 7 8 0 5 7 8 0 7 5 6 9 3 *